ROXY ANN

Roxy Ann's Adventures:
Day at Home

Illustrations inspired by:
Emma Testa

BY MANDI DAVEY

MILTON & HUGO L.L.C.
4407 Park Ave., Suite 5
Union City, NJ 07087, USA

Website: www. miltonandhugo.com
Hotline: 1- 888-778-0033
Email: info@miltonandhugo.com

Ordering Information:
Quantity sales. Special discounts are available on quantity purchases by corporations, associations, and others. For details, contact the publisher at the address above.

ISBN-13:   979-8-89285-471-9   [Paperback Edition]
              979-8-89285-771-0   [Hardback Edition]
              979-8-89285-470-2   [Digital Edition]

Rev. date: 11/26/2025

ROXY ANN

MANDI DAVEY

Hey Roxy, Mom is leaving to go to work. (giving some much-needed patting on the head and hugs goodbye). When I get back, I'll take you outside again. I love you so much and I will see you soon.

As mom leaves the house Roxy quickly jumps up onto the back of the couch to the window. Roxy watches out the window as Mom gets into her car and waves goodbye.

4

"Yawning" Roxy looks out the window, mom is not back yet. Roxy jumps down from the couch and heads to the kitchen to get a snack. She then drinks some water.

Since Mom is gone, I think
I will take a nap!

Roxy makes her way back to the living room and jumps back up to the couch to look out the window to see if Mom is back yet. As Roxy sits in her spot on the back of the couch waiting patiently for Mom to get home, she makes nose prints on the window.

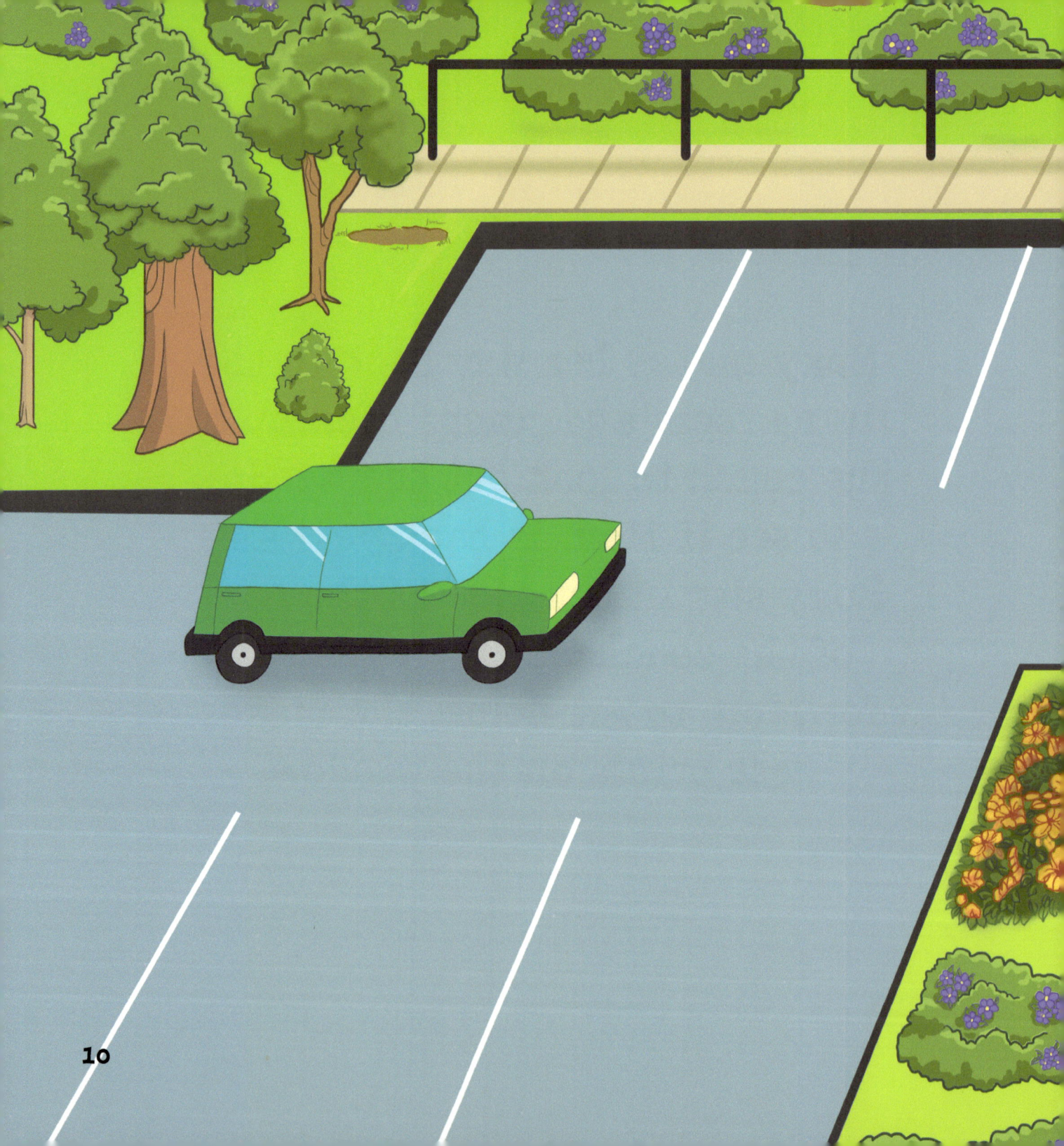

Suddenly Roxy sees Mom
driving the car! Roxy gets so
excited and starts to jump up
and down. Here comes Mom she
is getting out of the car now
OH BOY! She's waving to Me!

Roxy jumps up off the back of the couch down to the cushions and "bolts" for the door. As Roxy waits for Mom to unlock the door and open it, she makes little crying noises of anticipation.

Finally, the door opens and there is Mom. Roxy cannot wait to get her hugs and kisses from mom.

Mom, I have waited for you all day can we go outside for my walk now? Oh, Roxy, I have missed you so much let me put my purse down and get your leash.

Are you ready Peanut?
let's go for your walk.

Follow me on Instagram:

@ROXYANN23

SCAVENGER HUNT

Look for the following:

1.

2.

3.

4.

5.

6.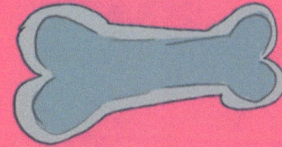

7.

8.

www.ingramcontent.com/pod-product-compliance
Lightning Source LLC
Chambersburg PA
CBHW041558040426
42447CB00002B/216